W9-BZB-228

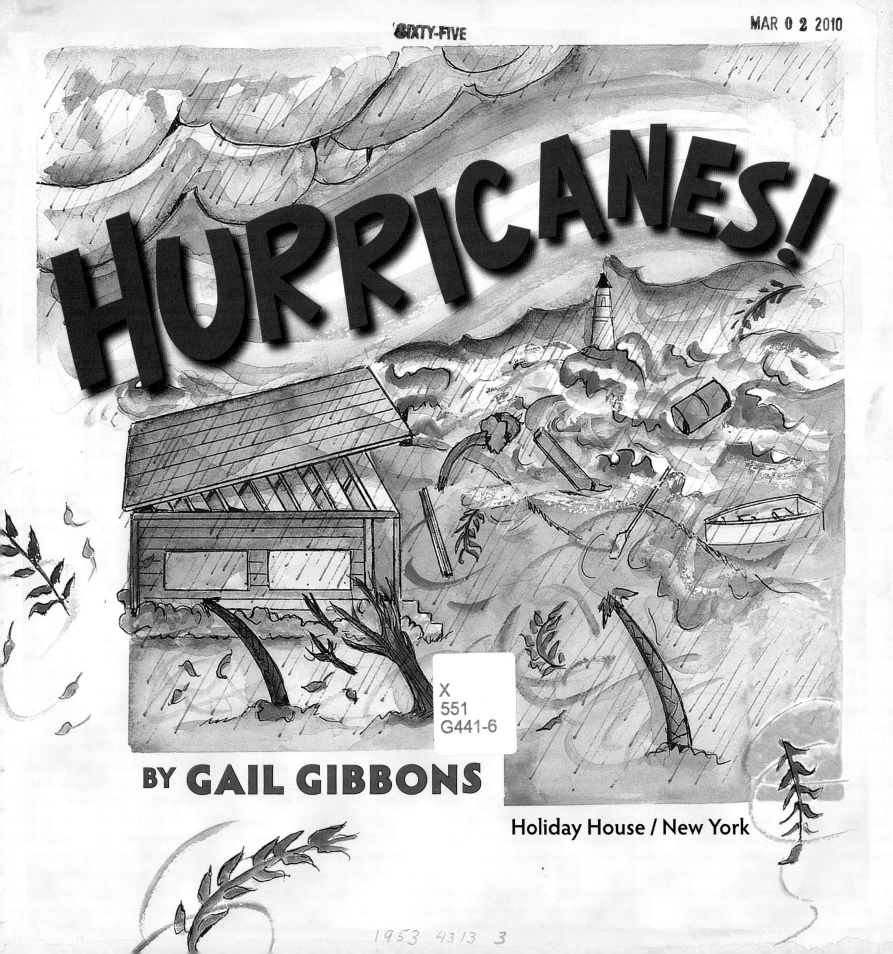

HURRICANES!

BY GAIL GIBBONS

Holiday House / New York

To "Hurricane" Donna

Special thanks to Eric Evenson of the National Weather Service, South Burlington, Vermont.

Copyright © 2009 by Gail Gibbons
All Rights Reserved
HOLIDAY HOUSE is registered in the U.S.
Patent and Trademark Office.
Printed in the United States of America
www.holidayhouse.com
First Edition
1 3 5 7 9 10 8 6 4 2
Library of Congress Cataloging-in-Publication Data
Gibbons, Gail.
Hurricanes! / by Gail Gibbons. — 1st ed.
p. cm.
ISBN 978-0-8234-2233-3 (hardcover)
1. Hurricanes—Juvenile literature. I. Title.
QC944.2.G53 2009
551.55'2—dc22
2009008761

HURRICANE comes from Hurakan, the name for the ancient Mayan god of the big winds.

The winds are howling, the rain is pouring down, violent waves are crashing onto the shore. A dangerous spinning storm has formed over tropical waters. It is a hurricane.

CUMULONIMBUS CLOUDS

EVAPORATES means that water turns into moist air.

F = Fahrenheit
C = Celsius

All hurricanes form over tropical waters. Warm water evaporates and rises into the atmosphere. The warm moist air spins upward, creating a draft that sucks up more moisture. If the water temperature is more than 81°F (27.2° C), the cycle continues. Winds get stronger. As the moist air rises, cumulonimbus (KYOOM-you-low-NIM-bus) clouds are formed.

mph = miles per hour
kph = kilometers per hour

CONDENSATION occurs when the moist, warm air cools and turns into rain.

The rising air creates even more of an updraft. Even more moisture rises, creating even larger cumulonimbus clouds that hold even more water. The spinning of the air accelerates. Even larger groups of cumulonimbus clouds continue to build up. Condensation causes rain. When the speed of the wind reaches 74 mph (119.1 kph), the storm is classified as a hurricane.

EYE

EYEWALL

EYEWALL

Most hurricanes are about 100 miles (160.9 kilometers) to 300 miles (482.8 kilometers) wide. The center of a hurricane is called the eye, which is clear and calm. It may be 10 to 20 miles (16.1 to 32.2 kilometers) wide. The strongest winds in a hurricane are those closest to the eye of the storm. This area is called the eyewall.

UNITED STATES

ATLANTIC OCEAN

GULF OF MEXICO

BAHAMAS

CUBA

CARIBBEAN SEA

DOMINICAN REPUBLIC

VIRGIN ISLANDS

HAITI

JAMAICA

PUERTO RICO

BARBADOS

TRINIDAD & TOBAGO

COLOMBIA

VENEZUELA

USA

ATLANTIC OCEAN

MEXICO

CARIBBEAN

AFRICA

EQUATOR

SOUTH AMERICA

Most hurricanes form over the Atlantic Ocean north of the equator. They usually last about a week and travel on a course that is very difficult to predict.

Many hurricanes have devastated cities and towns with strong winds. Usually there are heavy rains. Sometimes there is hail. Storm surges cause the greatest damage. They are huge walls of water forced up out of the sea, devastating everything in their path and on occasion altering the shoreline itself.

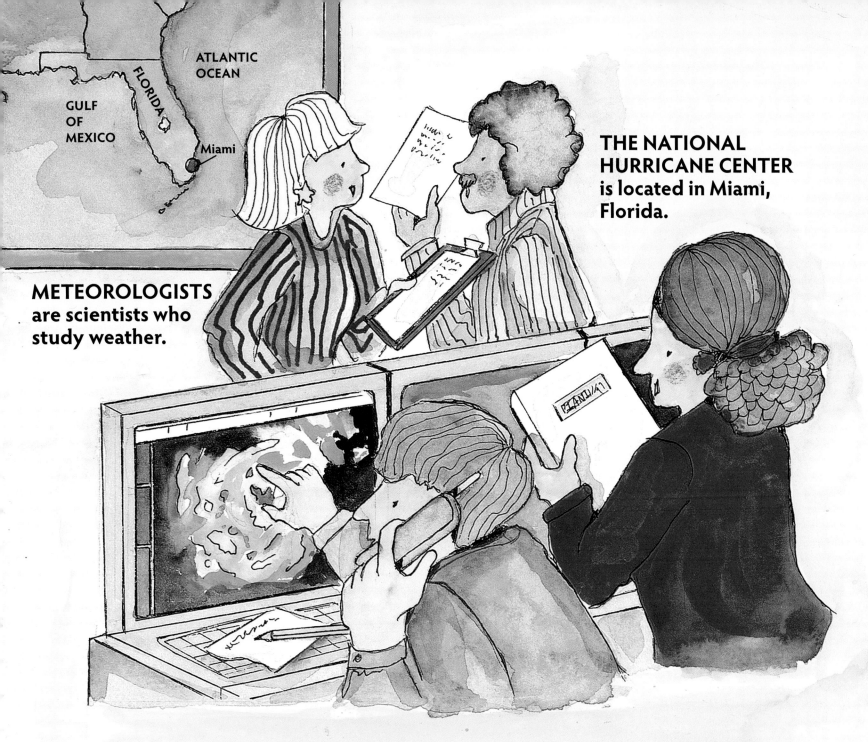

ATLANTIC
OCEAN

FLORIDA

GULF
OF
MEXICO

Miami

THE NATIONAL HURRICANE CENTER is located in Miami, Florida.

METEOROLOGISTS are scientists who study weather.

In 1972, Herbert Saffir and Robert Simpson developed the Saffir-Simpson Hurricane Scale. This scale ranks hurricanes in categories of 1 to 5. It has permitted meteorologists at the National Hurricane Center to predict the likely impact of an approaching hurricane.

CATEGORY 1 HURRICANES

Category 1 hurricanes have wind speeds between 74 mph (119.1 kph) and 95 mph (152.9 kph). There may be a storm surge of up to 5 feet (1.5 meters).

There is some damage to trees and small buildings.

CATEGORY 3 HURRICANES

Category 3 hurricanes have wind speeds between 111 mph (178.6 kph) and 130 mph (209.7 kph). There may be a storm surge of up to 12 feet (3.7 meters).

Trees are uprooted. Large cars and trucks are swept away. There is extensive damage to buildings and boats.

CATEGORY 4 HURRICANES

Category 4 hurricanes have wind speeds between 131 mph (210.8 kpm) and 155 mph (249 kpm). There may be a storm surge of up to to 18 feet (5.5 meters).

The damage is devastating. Buildings suffer extreme damage. Roads and bridges are washed away. Boats are tossed about like toys.

CATEGORY 5 HURRICANES

Category 5 hurricanes have winds greater than 155 mph (249 kph). Winds have been recorded as high as 318 mph (511.8 kph). Storm surges may be greater than 18 feet (5.5 meters).

There is massive flooding and destruction.

HURRICANES COME ASHORE ...

ATLANTIC OCEAN

NC

SC

MS AL GA

TX

LA

FL

New Orleans

Galveston

Miami

MEXICO

GULF OF
MEXICO

CARIBBEAN SEA

Most hurricanes do their damage in the Caribbean and along the Gulf coast and the southeast coast of the United States.

SOUTH AMERICA

EQUATOR

Most hurricanes are Category 1 or 2. Category 5 hurricanes are rare and have reached land on an average of once every five years.

SOME HURRICANES THROUGHOUT HISTORY
GALVESTON September 8, 1900

TEXAS

Galveston

MEXICO

GULF OF MEXICO

In 1900 the biggest city in Texas was Galveston. On September 8, a huge hurricane struck. The storm surge was 20 feet (6.1 meters) high. It totally destroyed the city, killing about 12,000 people. Scientists later classified it a Category 5 hurricane.

HURRICANE ANDREW August 24, 1992

ATLANTIC OCEAN

GULF OF MEXICO

FL

Miami

After crossing the Bahamas, Hurricane Andrew hit Florida south of Miami with winds up to 195 mph (313.8 kph). At that time it was the costliest hurricane in U.S. history. Most of the damage was done by the fierce winds. Originally classified a Category 4 hurricane, it was reclassified a Category 5.

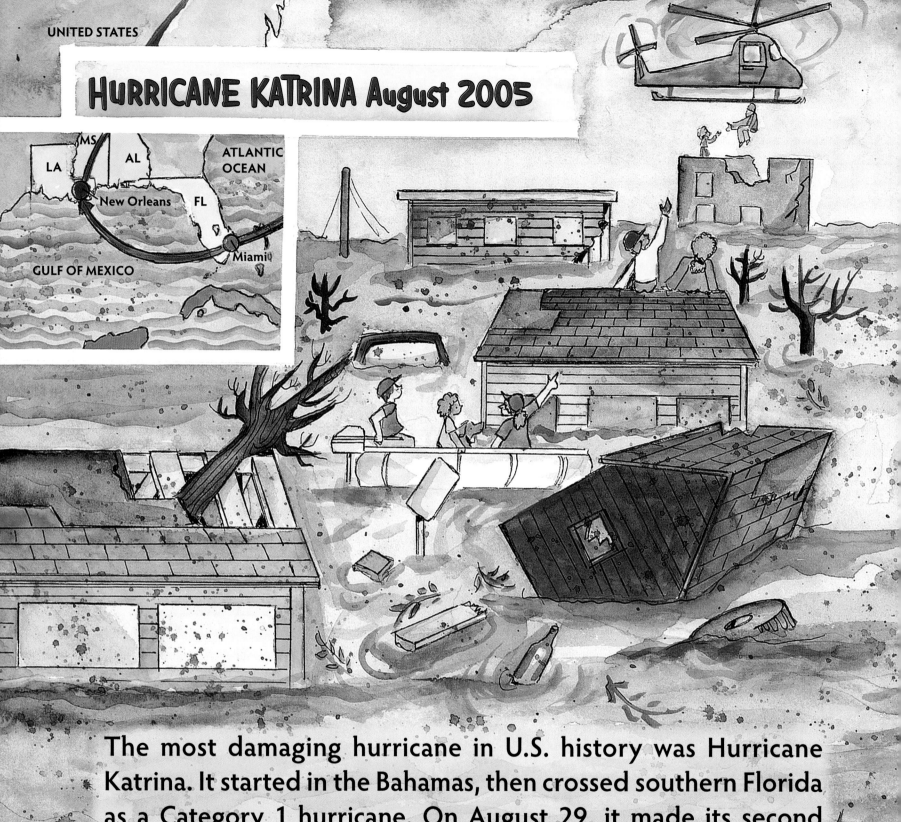

HURRICANE KATRINA August 2005

UNITED STATES

MS
LA
AL
ATLANTIC OCEAN
New Orleans
FL
Miami
GULF OF MEXICO

The most damaging hurricane in U.S. history was Hurricane Katrina. It started in the Bahamas, then crossed southern Florida as a Category 1 hurricane. On August 29, it made its second landfall in New Orleans as a Category 5 Hurricane.

EVACUATE means to leave and seek safety in another place.

EVACUATION ROUTE

Storm surges resulted in the flooding of 80 percent of New Orleans. More than one million people had to evacuate, and nearly 1,800 people lost their lives. Catastrophic damage was done all along the coastlines of Louisiana, Mississippi, and Alabama.

FORECASTING AND TRACKING HURRICANES

WEATHER
SATELLITE

Meteorologists gather information about hurricanes from many sources. Satellites measure the size of a hurricane and can help tell how fast and in what direction a hurricane is moving.

An airplane passes through one side of a hurricane, then through the eye and out through the other side.

Hurricane Hunters are members of the Air Force Reserve.

U.S. AIR FORCE

Airplanes are flown into hurricanes by pilots known as Hurricane Hunters. Special instruments on the planes measure wind speeds, temperatures, air pressures, and the amount of moisture in the clouds.

All of the storm's details are gathered and fed into computers which are preprogrammed with computer models of previous storms. This helps scientists make a new computer model that predicts the size and strength of the storm and what land may be in its path.

A STORM WATCH is a notice that tells people in a certain area that a hurricane might hit within thirty-six hours.

One flag means STORM WATCH.

A HURRICANE WARNING is a notice telling people that a hurricane is likely to hit within twenty-four hours.

Two flags mean HURRICANE WARNING.

These predictions help determine if an area will need to be evacuated. When necessary, the National Hurricane Center will issue storm watches and hurricane warnings that are made public on radio and television. The U.S. Coast Guard raises flags.

Many hurricanes may be forming at one time.
Giving them names makes it easier to track them.

In 1953 weather officials started naming hurricanes after women, with the first storm of the season being given a woman's name beginning with the letter *A*, the second storm a name beginning with the letter *B*, and so on. In 1979 men's names started to be used as well. The names of some of the worst storms have been retired and will not be used again. Andrew and Katrina are two of these.

WHEN A HURRICANE IS APPROACHING. . .

There should be a plan to evacuate. Everyone should know the route.

Cover the windows of your house with plywood to prevent flying glass.

Have a battery-powered radio on hand to hear all alerts.

Turn off the electricity to your house before you evacuate.

Select a person outside the hurricane area who can inform other family members of your status.

Take care of your family pets.

Pick up loose items in your yard and put them away. They can become dangerous in strong winds.

TRY TO HAVE AN ADULT HELP YOU.

Make sure the family supply kit is ready.

✓ WATER
✓ NONPERISHABLE FOODS
✓ FLASHLIGHT
✓ FRESH BATTERIES
✓ FIRST-AID KIT
✓ BATTERY-POWERED RADIO
✓ RAINWEAR

MORE INTERESTING FACTS . . .

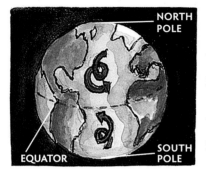

Hurricanes north of the equator rotate <u>counterclockwise</u>. Hurricanes south of the equator rotate <u>clockwise</u>.

The deadliest storm on record is a cyclone in Bangladesh in 1970. More than 300,000 people died.

Cyclones are hurricane-like storms that form over the Pacific Ocean.

The evaporation of about two billion tons (1.8 billion metric tons) of water a day can occur while a hurricane is building up over the ocean.

Typhoons are hurricane-like storms that form over the Indian Ocean.

WEBSITES

In the United States:
http://www.nhc.noaa.gov/

In Canada:
http://www.atl.ec.gc.ca/
weather/hurricane/

Select: *English* or *French*

Signs mark evacuation routes.